Telephone Sk
at Work

THIS IS THE PROPERTY OF
THE TRAINING LIBRARY

NORTHERN EXAMINATIONS
AND ASSESSMENT BOARD

Telephone Skills at Work

JUDITH E. FISHER, Ph.D.

The Business Skills Express Series

BUSINESS ONE IRWIN/MIRROR PRESS
Burr Ridge, Illinois
New York, New York
Boston, Massachusetts

© RICHARD D. IRWIN, INC., 1994

Mirror Press: David R. Helmstadter
                             Carla F. Tishler

Editor-in-chief: Jeffrey A. Krames
Project editor: Stephanie M. Britt
Production manager: Diane Palmer
Designer: Jeanne M. Rivera
Art coordinator: Heather Burbridge
Illustrator: Boston Graphics, Inc.
Compositor: TCSystems, Inc.
Typeface: 12/14 Criterion
Printer: Malloy Lithographing, Inc.

Library of Congress Cataloging-in-Publication Data

Fisher, Judith E.
      Using the telephone for business results / Judith E. Fisher.
          p.   cm.—(Business skills express)
      ISBN 1-55623-858-4
        1. Telephone in business.   I. Title.
    HF5541.T4F58   1994
    651.7′3—dc20   93–7

Printed in the United States of America
1 2 3 4 5 6 7 8 9 0   ML   0 9 8 7 6 5 4 3

PREFACE

Q: "What does it take to run a business?"

A: "A telephone and someone to use it effectively!"

This may be an exaggeration, but it clearly points to the facts. The telephone is the most popular, most widely used business tool. It's no surprise that telephone skills are critical for success in business.

This book focuses on business telephone skills. Whether you work the phone all day—taking orders, selling, handling requests—or simply use the telephone for routine business communications, this book has something for you. If you're new to the business world, it can help you learn the essential telephone skills you'll need on the job. If you're experienced in business, it can help you refine your telephone skills and make your work easier.

Chapters 1 and 2 discuss the role of the telephone in business and the challenges of communicating via the telephone. Chapter 3 examines three key telephone skills: listening, questioning, and speaking. Chapter 4 offers business telephone tips. Chapters 5, 6, and 7 focus on handling various types of incoming calls. Chapter 8 deals with outbound calls for sales and service. The book ends with a review test and recommendations for sharpening your skills.

This book is designed to be used in many different ways. You might be using it as part of a training session at work, or you might be using it in an off-site seminar, or workshop. In those situations, your group leader will give you specific directions on how to use this book.

You might be using this book as part of your own personal job-skills improvement plan. The book is designed for independent self-study, where you are in control of the learning experience. There's no one looking over your shoulder. You decide which chapters of the book you want to tackle. You decide when, where, and how long to study.

To make the most of this learning experience:

- Schedule some uninterrupted time. Set aside half an hour, or tell yourself to finish a chapter you've selected.
- Eliminate distractions.
- Work through this book with a pen or pencil. Read the text passages and do the exercises. Write your answers and record your thoughts in the book. Take notes in the margins or highlight important ideas.
- Ask yourself these kinds of questions: How does this idea fit in with my job? How can I apply this technique? How could I adapt these ideas or techniques to fit my job?

Make the most of this opportunity to put your telephone skills to work for you!

Judith E. Fisher

ABOUT THE AUTHOR

Judith E. Fisher, Ph. D., is President of Education and Training Consultants, Inc., in Riverview, Florida. As a consultant, Dr. Fisher specializes in design, development, and production of education and training materials for the adult learner in business and industry. Her client roster includes Hilton Hotels, Inter-Continental Hotels, Marriott Hotels, MCI, Northern Telecom, Xerox, and IBM. Dr. Fisher is the recipient of several awards, including the National Endowment for the Humanities Fellowship and appointment to Outstanding Educators of America. She completed her doctoral work in Instructional Design and Development.

ABOUT BUSINESS ONE IRWIN

Business One Irwin is the nation's premier publisher of business books. As a Times Mirror company, we work closely with Times Mirror training organizations, including Zenger-Miller, Inc., Learning International, Inc., and Kaset International, to serve the training needs of business and industry.

About the Business Skills Express Series

This expanding series of authoritative, concise, and fast-paced books delivers high quality training on key business topics at a remarkably affordable cost. The series will help managers, supervisors, and front line personnel in organizations of all sizes and types hone their business skills while enhancing job performance and career satisfaction.

Business Skills Express books are ideal for employee seminars, independent self-study, on-the-job training, and classroom-based instruction. Express books are also convenient-to-use references at work.

CONTENTS

Self-Assessment

How do you feel about your business telephone skills? Here's an opportunity to analyze your strengths and weaknesses. Read each statement; then beside each statement, mark the appropriate space. Be honest with yourself!

	Almost Always	Sometimes	Almost Never
1. I answer the telephone promptly.	_____	_____	_____
2. I have a standard way of answering the phone at work.	_____	_____	_____
3. I avoid making personal calls from my business telephone.	_____	_____	_____
4. I identify myself when I answer the phone at work.	_____	_____	_____
5. I try to make my calls brief and businesslike.	_____	_____	_____
6. I have a process model that I use to help handle problem callers.	_____	_____	_____
7. I am an excellent listener.	_____	_____	_____
8. I speak clearly and carefully in telephone conversations.	_____	_____	_____
9. My speaking voice is pleasant.	_____	_____	_____
10. I am a skilled questioner.	_____	_____	_____
11. I use the telephone every day to speak with customers or clients.	_____	_____	_____
12. I know how to overcome the challenges and limitations of telephone communications.	_____	_____	_____
13. I can comfortably use all of the features of the telephone system at work.	_____	_____	_____
14. I use a consistent form for taking telephone messages.	_____	_____	_____
15. I always organize my thoughts before I make a call.	_____	_____	_____

As you probably surmised, there are no right or wrong answers. Your goal is to change all your "no" responses to "yes" responses by the time you've worked through this book. Good luck!

Telephone Skills at Work

1 | Business Use of the Telephone

This chapter will help you to:

- Describe the importance of the telephone in business.
- Analyze your own business telephone use.

THE ROLE OF THE TELEPHONE IN BUSINESS

The telephone, invented in 1876 by Alexander Graham Bell, made an immediate and tremendous impact on society. Communication has never been the same since.

From Luxury to Necessity

The first long-distance call in 1878—a call from Boston to Providence, only 45 miles away—sparked the development of better telephone technologies. The arrival of mechanical telephone switching in 1879 reduced dependence on human operators. Telephone wires linking house to house and business to business suddenly became status symbols. The invention of the telephone literally changed the world.

It's been more than a century since Bell's first telephone. The telephone has evolved from a status symbol into a utility. We no longer think of the telephone as a luxury—it is a necessity. Fast, direct, and convenient, the telephone has become the most popular, most widely used means of electronic communication in the world.

The Telephone in Business

Which is the most popular means of communication in business: a meeting, a business letter, a facsimile transmission, or a computer data transfer? None! It's the telephone!

1

Billions of business telephone calls are made each year. It's hard to imagine a business operating effectively without the telephone. When telephone service is interrupted—even for a short time—businesses complain loudly about their losses.

Without telephones:

- Orders would be received by mail or delivery services.
- Customers would have to travel to the business location just to ask questions or to get information.
- Workers on different floors or in different buildings would have to meet face-to-face for every discussion or send endless rounds of memos.

Without the telephone, business would be a mess. Commerce would literally grind to a halt. The slowness of written communications and the time and costs associated with in-person meetings would soon become intolerable. In fact, we've had reliable business telephone service for so long that it has become an integral part of the way we do business.

■ T h i n k   a b o u t   I t

Take a minute to think about your job and your business use of the telephone.

1. How many times during an average workday do you use the telephone? _____

2. What kinds of business activities do you typically handle over the telephone? (Refer to the list in the Chapter Checkpoints for some ideas.)

   _____
   _____
   _____
   _____
   _____
   _____
   _____

3. Imagine you are going to be promoted. Think about the job or position you'd like to have.

   Will that job involve using the telephone? _____

   Will it require more or less telephone use? _____

   Will it involve other (or additional) business activities to be handled over the telephone? If so, make a list. _____

   _____
   _____
   _____
   _____
   _____

Chapter Checkpoints

Who Uses the Telephone?

Review the two lists below. Check off the job titles or positions that typically use the telephone on the job. Then check off the business activities that are done over the telephone.

Jobs/Positions	Business Activities
☐ Secretary.	☐ Taking dictation.
☐ Data-entry clerk.	☐ Servicing customer accounts.
☐ Receptionist.	☐ Setting up appointments.
☐ Order entry clerk.	☐ Taking customer orders.
☐ Service representatives.	☐ Answering customer inquiries.
☐ President or chief executive.	☐ Selling.
☐ Sales representative.	☐ Providing information.
☐ Billing clerk.	☐ Setting up meetings.
☐ Inventory manager.	☐ Handling complaints.
☐ Bookkeeper.	☐ Giving directions.
☐ Payroll clerk.	☐ Discussing issues.
☐ Accounts payable clerk.	☐ Leaving messages.
☐ Financial officer.	☐ Providing customer support.
☐ V. P. of manufacturing.	☐ Clarifying situations.
☐ V. P. of operations.	☐ Sharing ideas.
☐ Training director.	☐ Confirming arrangements.
☐ Shipping clerk.	☐ Making travel plans.
☐ Warehouse worker.	☐ Ordering supplies.
☐ Route salesperson.	☐ Obtaining vendor services.

Checkpoint Feedback

How many did you check off? You probably have the point.

What jobs or positions require telephone use? **All of them!**

What kinds of business activities are conducted over the phone? **All kinds!**

2 | The Challenge of Telephone Communication

This chapter will help you to:

- Explain how the communications process works.
- Define the four parts in the communications process.
- Identify common telephone communications problems.

A SIMPLE COMMUNICATIONS MODEL

Telephone skills are communication skills. This chapter examines a model of the communications process and notes the special challenges associated with telephone communications. It sets up a logical framework for the telephone skills you'll be reviewing later.

Human communication is a process transferring information (thoughts, ideas, opinions, and attitudes) from one person to another. The simplest communication process always involves four main parts: a sender, a message, a channel, and a receiver.

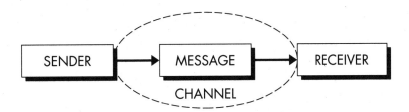

- A sender is the person who has information to convey to another person.
- The message is the information to be communicated.
- A channel is the means or medium of communication. The channel might be telephone wires in person-to-person communication, a printed page of a book or letter, a video

transmission via satellite link or cable, or even data transmission over wires from computer to computer.

- A receiver is the person who takes in the information that is sent.

Applying the Communication Model

Think about the communication model for a moment. It covers almost every type of human communication you can imagine. Our area of interest is person-to-person communication, particularly telephone conversations. Think of the communication model in that context.

The model certainly fits two people talking face-to-face. The sender is the speaker, and the receiver is the listener. The message is the words that are spoken, plus the visual cues the speaker provides, and the channel is the air.

SENDER = SPEAKER　　**VISUAL BARRIER**　　**RECEIVER = LISTENER**

The model also fits the telephone conversation, as in the diagram. Notice an important difference. The channel in telephone communication is the telephone wire. The sender and receiver can no longer see each other. The channel prevents them from using visual cues—facial expressions, body language, and gestures—to help convey and interpret the message.

By using the communication model, you can see how telephone communication differs from face-to-face conversation. The channel is different (wires) and the message is different (no visual cues). The telephone requires extra effort for effective communication.

PROBLEMS IN TELEPHONE COMMUNICATION

"I've been using the telephone my whole life. It's not really hard to do. Why did I never recognize challenges or problems?" We've become creatures of our telephone habits. Having made and received countless phone calls, it's easy to assume that our telephone skills are adequate. Most people never think about the special challenges of telephone communications. But, if you understand the problems that can arise in telephone calling, you are better prepared to solve them.

When all the parts of the communications process work effectively together, telephone communication is clear and useful. Sometimes even a well-practiced communication process can go awry. Problems can occur in any of the four parts of:

1. Trouble sending: The sender mumbles his or her words, speaks in an obscure language, or whispers. What happens to the message? Will it be received?

2. Trouble with the message: The message is confusing, disorganized, or irrational. Is it likely that the receiver will understand what is being communicated?

3. Trouble with the channel: There is noise or interference in the channel. Will the message be transmitted effectively? Will it be received?

4. Trouble with the receiver: The receiver is not listening closely, has fallen asleep, or is distracted. Will the message be understood?

■ Think about It

Have any of these typical telephone communications problems happened to you? Check those you've experienced; then add any others you've known.

Problems Related to the Sender

☐ The sender speaks too softly. You have to ask the sender to speak up.

☐ The sender talks a mile a minute. You have to ask the sender to slow down.

☐ The sender talks so slowly you want to fill in with your own ideas or anticipate what is going to be said.

☐ The speaker mumbles.

☐ The sender talks so loudly you have to hold the telephone handset away from your ear.

Other problems: _____

_____

_____

_____

Problems Related to the Message

☐ The speaker uses slang vocabulary that you cannot decode.

☐ The speaker uses so many five-dollar words that you don't know what is being said.

☐ The speaker repeats the message too many times.

☐ The information is disorganized or the message is confusing.

☐ The message is in a foreign language that you do not understand.

☐ The speaker assumes you already know the information or have background related to it.

☐ The information is too detailed for effective telephone communication.

Other problems: _____

_____

_____

_____

Problems Related to the Channel

- ☐ There is static or buzzing on the line.
- ☐ There is background noise coming from the sender's location (radio, stereo, or TV).
- ☐ The connection breaks, leaving you with a dial tone.
- ☐ There is an echo on the line.

Other problems: _____
_____
_____
_____

Problems Related to the Receiver

- ☐ The receiver doesn't acknowledge that the message is being understood.
- ☐ The receiver doesn't engage in a two-way conversation.
- ☐ The receiver is distracted and stops paying attention to the sender.
- ☐ The receiver gets sidetracked or goes astray.
- ☐ The receiver is conducting another conversation at the same time.
- ☐ The receiver is not listening.
- ☐ The receiver cannot understand or decifer the message.

Other problems: _____
_____
_____
_____

You've undoubtedly had many of the problems in the list, and you probably added a few examples of your own.

Why focus on the potential problems of telephone communication? A telephone conversation is a complex process with special challenges. If not managed well, it can—and will—break down. If any part of the process is out of balance, the telephone conversation will fail to achieve its purpose.

In a personal telephone call, you usually don't need to worry about these elements. In a business situation, telephone communication is much more critical. Effective business use of the telephone is much more than simply dialing a number and opening a dialogue.

Chapter Checkpoints

Review the key points in the quiz below. When you have finished the quiz, check your answers.

1. There are four main parts in a simplified communication model. Name and describe each of them in your own words.

_____

_____

_____

_____

_____

_____

_____

_____

_____

_____

_____

_____

_____

2. What is the most popular means of communication in business?

_____

3. Explain why telephone communication has become an integral part of the way business is done.

_____

_____

_____

4. Describe how telephone communication differs from face-to-face communication.

_____

_____

Checkpoint Feedback

Check your answers by referring to the suggested responses.

1. *Sender*—the person who has information to convey.
   Message—the information to be communicated.
   Channel—the means or medium of communication.
   Receiver—the person who takes in the information that is sent.

2. The telephone.

3. The telephone is fast, direct, and immediate. It is also inexpensive. Businesses have had reliable telephone service for so long that businesses cannot function without telephones.

4. There are two main differences. In telephone conversations, the channel is a telephone wire, not just the air between two people. Also, there is a visual barrier, so we don't have facial expressions and body language to help us communicate.

3 | Key Telephone Skills

This chapter will help you to:

- Apply listening skills effectively.
- Use direct and indirect questions in business telephone calls.
- Examine the factors that influence the speaking voice.
- Analyze your own telephone speaking voice.

THREE KEY SKILLS

Three key telephone skills are necessary for business telephone calls:

- Listening.
- Questioning.
- Speaking.

These three skills are the basis for audible human communication and form the core of any conversation. Mastery of these key skills guarantees improved business telephone communication.

In this chapter, we'll take a closer look at each of these three skills. Some of the information presented may be news to you, while other ideas may help refresh your skills. In either case, it's always a good idea to start with the basics.

| LISTENING | QUESTIONING | SPEAKING |

FUNDAMENTAL TELEPHONE SKILLS

Listening

Listening is not the same as *hearing*. Hearing is a physical ability that requires no intellectual effort. As long as you are physically equipped to receive sounds, you can hear. Listening, on the other hand, is more than simply hearing sounds. It is an active process that requires both hearing and thinking.

Listening during a Conversation.   A conversation implies a two-way exchange of information. In Chapter 2, you saw a one-way flow of information illustrated in the communication model. In real-life conversations, of course, the sender and receiver continually switch roles. People engaged in conversation spend some of their time talking (sending information) and some of their time listening (receiving information). Normally, one person speaks while the other listens, and vice versa.

In an average telephone conversation, *you can expect to spend about 50 percent of your time listening.* Why does that obvious fact seem startling? When we think about using the telephone, we think about talking. We really don't think about the other side of the conversational coin—listening. Listening is a critical communication skill that can really make a difference in your ability to do business on the telephone.

What Happens When You Don't Listen?   Most of us tend to be impatient. We go through the motions of listening because we can hardly wait for our turn to talk.

An initial comment made by the speaker often triggers a clever, on-target response in your mind. Most of us have a tendency to seem to be listening by making appropriate facial expressions or by staying quiet during a telephone conversation. We get so wrapped up in thinking about our response that we often fail to listen. That can be disastrous in a business telephone call.

Some serious risks are associated with failing to listen during telephone conversations. *When you don't listen effectively, you may . . .*

- Misunderstand the speaker's problem or concern.
- Jump to conclusions without knowing all the facts.
- Give incorrect information to the caller.
- Confuse the caller with an inappropriate response.
- Appear to be rushing the speaker and cutting off conversation.
- Fail to understand the business situation.
- Misinterpret the speaker's comments.

Do you want to take those risks? Will your co-workers and customers be impressed with your telephone skills?

H i n t s

Time Out

Time out . . . for some words of wisdom from the American author and humorist, Ambrose Bierce. He offers this definition in *The Devil's Dictionary.*

"Bore: A person who talks when you wish him to listen."

Think about your business telephone conversations. Do you ever wait impatiently when someone else talks too much? Do you always follow the general rule of "talk less and listen more"? Would your business contacts have reason to think of you as a telephone bore?

Guidelines for Better Listening

Here are six simple guidelines to improve your listening skills. Think about how you might apply each of them in your business telephone conversations.

3

1. Listen for understanding. Your mind can process information faster than a speaker can send it. That means you'll need to develop discipline in listening. Concentrate on important points. Summarize and repeat them in your mind as the other person speaks so that you reinforce your understanding.
2. Verify what you think you heard. Repeat or rephrase what you think you heard; then ask the speaker to verify the accuracy of your understanding.
3. Listen for expression. In a telephone conversation, you don't have the benefit of visual cues, so pay special attention to the speaker's vocal and verbal expression.
4. Notice what is not being said. Listen for omissions. Sometimes the unspoken message can be very important! Be aware of evasiveness, hesitancy, or tentativeness.
5. Listen objectively. Keep an open mind during the telephone conversation. Don't prejudge. Don't try to guess what the speaker will say next. Control your own reactions if and when the conversation touches your emotions.
6. Stay involved in the conversation. Keep your attention focused. It's easy to let your mind stray, particularly when you don't have eye contact and face-to-face presence to keep you interested. Don't turn off your attention or let your attention wander during the call. Concentrate.

Think about It: Practicing Listening for Meaning

In thinking about effective listening, focus on the intellectual effort it requires. Listening is an active skill, not a passive one. During your next business telephone call, remember to listen for meaning by asking yourself the following questions. If necessary, take brief notes during the telephone call.

- What is being said?

  _____

  _____

- Is it fact or opinion?

  _____

  _____

- What was actually meant?

  _____

  _____

- Was there a hidden meaning?

  _____

  _____

- Why did the person say that?

  _____

  _____

- Does he or she believe what was said? Do you believe it?

  _____

  _____

- Is the person holding back? Why? What?

  _____

  _____

- Does the information have an emotional impact?

  _____

  _____

Questioning

A business telephone call is a dialogue—a two-way exchange of information. When you are not listening, chances are you will either be explaining something or asking questions to obtain information. Later, we'll talk about making explanations, but let's concentrate on the second key telephone skill.

Questioning as a Telephone Skill.   Questioning is a systematic process that enables you to discover information.

In business telephone calls, ask questions to accomplish two goals:

1. To get the information you need.
2. To verify or confirm information you've received.

3

Of course, you'll ask these questions in a conversational way. You don't want the conversation to turn into an interrogation!

There are two basic types of questions: *direct* and *indirect.*

Direct Questions.   Sometimes your telephone call will be designed to find out very specific pieces of information. In those instances, you need to ask a series of direct questions.

"What date have you selected for the regional meeting?"

"Will Mr. Jones be returning before 5 P.M. today?"

"Would you prefer the 6:00 flight or the 7:15?"

"Is the schedule all right with your team?"

"Are you authorized to make that decision?"

Direct questions are straightforward. They focus the conversation on a limited topic, and they obtain specific information. Direct questions (sometimes called closed questions) can be answered with a few words, such as a yes or no.

Indirect Questions.   In some telephone conversations, you need to uncover more general information, share ideas, or discuss opinions. For these situations, you would ask a series of indirect questions.

"Why have you chosen to stay with your present supplier?"

"What are your goals for this year?"

"How is your company organized?"

"Would you describe what happens in your department?"

"What is the purpose for the meeting?"

Indirect questions encourage general, wider-ranging responses. They open up avenues for further thought and discussion. Indirect questions (sometimes called open questions) cannot be answered with a word or two. They are designed to get the other person to talk freely, at some length, and in his or her own way.

Using Direct and Indirect Questions.   There are two types of questions often used in business telephone conversations. When is each type most appropriate? Here is a short summary.

Use direct questions: To discover specific information, come to an agreement, or confirm information received.

Use indirect questions: To determine needs, uncover problems, or understand issues or concerns.

Guidelines for Effective Questioning

Learning how to use questions effectively takes practice and guidelines.

1. Select appropriate questions. Plan a general line of questioning before you make the call. Ideally, you'll identify the information you need, then prepare questions to get the conversation rolling. You cannot anticipate every question, but you can make an educated guess.

2. Listen to the answers to your questions. Remember, questioning is one of the broader skills you use in a professional business conversation. Don't tie yourself too tightly to a strict line of questioning. Don't start forming your next question until you've listened to the answer to the last one. Be sure you don't answer the questions yourself.

3. Timing is important. In a telephone conversation, timing is everything. Avoid interrupting the conversational flow with a question out of context, but take advantage of conversational opportunities when they arise.

4. Continue questioning to confirm or verify information. Verifying is a special aspect of questioning. To verify, summarize what has been said (what you heard the other person say), then ask for confirmation with a question. Here are some examples.

Summarize:	"So the meeting will be in Dallas instead of Chicago . . .
Confirm:	. . . is that correct?"

Summarize:	"Your main concern is receiving proper credit for the returned merchandise . . .
Confirm:	. . . so when the credit shows up on your bill, you'll be satisfied, right?"

5. Avoid conducting an inquisition. There is a very delicate difference between an intense question and answer telephone call and an inquisition. If you get carried away firing questions, your listener will feel as though he or she is being grilled for information. It's best to acknowledge each answer briefly or comment in a relevant way before asking another question.

6. Don't get hung up on types of questions. Although it's useful to know and use the two types of questions, don't let yourself get hung up on the types themselves. After all, it is the answer—not the question—that is most important. Remember, your telephone contact may not respond in entirely predictable ways. Don't panic if he or she comes up with a one-word answer to your best indirect question! Take note of the information and realign your questions accordingly.

Hints

Time Out

Time out . . . for six important words. Every journalist knows that a story can be told in the answers to these questions:

Who? What? Where? When? How? Why?

As you get ready to gather information over the telephone, consider structuring your line of questioning around these six words.

Think about It: Developing a Line of Questioning

Develop a line of questioning for three situations. Describe a business telephone call situation in which you typically need to ask questions. Plan ahead by listing a few appropriate questions for each situation.

Example: Explain recent warranty changes to existing customers.
Q1: "Have you received the new warranty booklet we sent?"
Q2: "Do you understand the warranty has been extended?"
Q3: "Can I be of any further help at this time?"

1. Situation: _____

_____

Q1: _____

_____

Q2: _____

_____

Q3: _____

_____

2. Situation: _____

_____

Q1: _____

_____

Q2: _____

_____

Q3: _____

_____

3

3. Situation: _____

_____

Q1: _____

_____

Q2: _____

_____

Q3: _____

_____

Speaking

The person on the other end of the telephone line cannot see you. There is no visual imagery to assist communication, so the parties in a telephone conversation must rely entirely on sound. The speaking voices are the primary expression.

In business telephone calls, your speaking voice can be an asset or a liability. We would all like to have the resonant alto or baritone of the professional radio or TV announcer. Despite a lack of natural talent, we can all take steps to make sure our voices become a business asset.

What Factors Influence the Speaking Voice?   A number of variables directly affect vocal quality. There are three concrete variables and two less tangible traits.

Pitch in the speaking voice is much like pitch in singing.   Pitch ranges from low (bass) to high (soprano). In speaking voices, people show a general preference for the middle and lower ranges of the vocal scale. Low voices are regarded as signs of authority and trust. Higher voices, on the other hand, are often regarded as signs of immaturity or lack of experience. You may make a conscious effort to adjust your vocal pitch in either direction.

Test Your Pitch.   Read this sentence in your normal voice. Then mark a point on the scale that represents your pitch. Try this with a friend or two and ask them to mark where they think your pitch falls on the scale. Record yourself on a tape recorder, listen to yourself, and mark the scale again. You may be in for a surprise!

Low/Bass----- + ----- + ----- + ----- + ----- + -----High/Soprano

Speed is the rate at which you speak.   The range is from slow to fast, with the ideal somewhere in the middle. A fast talker appears impatient or seems to be steamrolling the conversation. If you talk too fast, your telephone contact may not be able to follow you. In contrast, a slow talker may appear to be a slow thinker, as well. If you talk too slowly, your conversational partner will be tempted to cut in, supply words, or otherwise hurry you.

Test Your Speed.   Read this paragraph aloud at your normal speed. Then mark a point on the scale that represents your speed. Again, try this with a couple of friends and ask them to mark where they think your speed registers on the scale or tape yourself. Do all measures agree?

Slow----- + ----- + ----- + ----- + ----- + ----- + ----- + -----Fast

Volume is the loudness of your voice.   The range is from soft to loud. Ideally, you'd want your voice in the middle of the range. What happens if you are talking too loudly or too softly? In either case, your telephone contact will find the conversation unpleasant and will be distracted by inappropriate volume.

Test Your Volume.   Again, read this sentence in your normal speaking voice or speak into a tape recorder. Mark your volume on the scale. Confirm your estimate by having a couple of friends mark the scale for you. Were you in the middle?

Quiet/Soft----- + ----- + ----- + ----- + ----- + -----Loud/Harsh

Pitch, speed, and volume are all concrete features of the human speaking voice. Next are two more traits that are not quite so easy to define.

Inflection is the modulation or change in a speaker's pitch or tone. Inflection gives your voice its personality. It provides the emphasis, interest, or accent that helps the listener understand your message. Inflection helps you show enthusiasm, interest, concern, and all the other possible human emotions.

A voice without inflection is described as monotone. A monotone voice is often associated with someone who is bored or uninterested. That's not an impression you want to make in a business telephone call. You want to use inflections to help communicate your message.

Try Some Inflections.   Read the following sentences aloud, using inflection to convey each of the following feelings or interpretations.

1. Normal   2. Excited   3. Afraid   4. Bored   5. Surprised

"I just heard the news on the radio. The merger is official."

Enunciation is the articulation or overall clarity of your speech. Garbled or indistinct speech annoys the listener. Your goal is always to speak clearly, pronouncing words correctly, and speaking distinctly. You want to avoid sounding stilted or affected, but you do want to strive for vocal clarity.

Putting the Factors Back Together.   We've dissected the speaking voice to look at five important variables:

- Pitch.
- Speed.
- Volume.
- Inflection.
- Enunciation.

There are other variables such as dialects or regional accents but we're focusing on the main ones. Let's put the five variables into perspective.

Your speaking voice reflects all of these variables. If you want to change your vocal quality, you might begin by changing one or more of these variables. Your general goal is to develop a professional, businesslike telephone voice that communicates your pleasant personality and positive attitude.

■ Think about It: Rating Your Own Skills

How would you rate your key telephone skills? Identify your strengths and weaknesses in listening, questioning, and speaking. Read each item and circle the letter that best describes your skill level.

P = Poor, G = Good, E = Excellent

P   G   E   1. Listening for understanding.

P   G   E   2. Interpreting what I heard.

P   G   E   3. Listening for expression.

P   G   E   4. Noticing what is not being said.

P   G   E   5. Staying attentive and involved in the telephone conversation.

P   G   E   6. Keeping an open mind during the conversation.

P   G   E   7. Verifying what I think I heard.

P   G   E   8. Formulating and using direct questions.

P   G   E   9. Formulating and using indirect questions.

P   G   E   10. Listening to the answers to my questions.

P   G   E   11. Planning a line of questioning before the telephone call.

P   G   E   12. Using timing to my advantage in the conversation.

P   G   E   13. Speaking in a medium pitch.

P   G   E   14. Speaking at a moderate rate.

P   G   E   15. Speaking with adequate volume.

P   G   E   16. Using inflection to show interest and personality.

P   G   E   17. Speaking and enunciating clearly.

Chapter Checkpoints

Fundamental Skills

Take a moment to check your understanding of the facts and ideas covered in this chapter of the book. Mark each sentence true or false. Then check your answers.

T F 1. A telephone conversation is a two-way exchange of information.

T F 2. Typically, the sender and receiver continually switch roles in a telephone conversation.

T F 3. In an average business telephone conversation, you spend 75 percent of your time talking and 25 percent of your time listening.

T F 4. A direct question is designed to discover specific information.

T F 5. An indirect question may be used to uncover general information, share ideas, or express opinions.

T F 6. To verify, first summarize or restate what you heard; then ask for confirmation with a question.

T F 7. A well-developed line of questioning anticipates every potential question that might be asked during a business telephone call.

T F 8. Pitch in the speaking voice ranges from low to high, with the ideal pitch being in the lower half of the range.

T F 9. It is not possible to make permanent changes in your natural speaking voice.

T F 10. A voice without inflection is a monotone.

T F 11. Inflection provides emphasis, interest, and feeling in the voice.

T F 12. Enunciation is the articulation of words and overall clarity of speech.

T F 13. You may choose to improve your speaking voice by manipulating your volume, speed, or pitch.

Checkpoint Feedback

Check your answers.

1. T
2. T
3. F
4. T
5. T
6. T
7. F
8. T
9. F
10. T
11. T
12. T
13. T

4 | Business Telephone Tips

This chapter will help you to:

- Use common telephone courtesy techniques during business calls.
- Develop strategies to work with internal and external customers.

BUSINESS TELEPHONE SYSTEMS

Do you want to use the telephone more effectively? Then start with the telephone system itself. If you work in a small business, the telephone system and equipment may work just like your home phone. In most larger businesses, the telephone systems are more sophisticated.

Business Features and Functions

Telephone companies offer a variety of equipment, systems, and special features. Although some advanced telephone functions are available for home use, many remain available only in business systems. The sophisticated features and functions of modern business telephone systems are designed to assist the businessperson in making and receiving calls more efficiently. However, in order to benefit from the features, you have to know how to use them first. That's not always as easy as it sounds. Although the phone is a simple instrument, the extra features and functions can be complicated.

The Office Expert

Is there someone in your office who is the telephone expert, a walking encyclopedia of telephone system information? The telephone expert seems to be the only person who knows how to use all of the complex features and functions of the ultramodern business telephone networks. The expert also is the only person who still has the user's guide or instruction manual that came with the phone system.

Unfortunately, the average business telephone user doesn't take time to master the finer points of telephone technology. Maybe no one ever trained the user on the phone system, or maybe it just seemed easier to rely on the office telephone expert. Your goal is mastery of the telephone system.

▣ Think about It

Directions: Analyze your business telephone system. Here is a checklist of common business telephone features to get you started. First, look over the list, check the features you have on your office telephone system, and add any features that are not listed. Second, for each feature or function you checked, assess your current level of confidence in using it. Mark each checked item as follows: H = High; M = Medium; L = Low.

_____ **1.** Call waiting.

_____ **2.** Cancel call waiting.

_____ **3.** Camp on.

_____ **4.** Call block (block selected numbers).

_____ **5.** Hold.

_____ **6.** Automatic last number redial.

_____ **7.** Automatic busy redial.

_____ **8.** VIP alert.

_____ **9.** Mute.

_____ **10.** Speaker phone.

_____ **11.** Conference calling or three-way calling.

_____ **12.** Multiple lines, numbers, or extensions.

_____ **13.** Speed dialing (automatic dialing).

_____ **14.** Call transferring.

_____ **15.** Message-waiting indicator.

_____ **16.** Dialing restrictions (control over outside calls).

_____ **17.** Internal network access codes.

_____ **18.** Call forwarding.

_____ **19.** Programmable number storage.

_____	**20.** Voice mail or messaging system.
_____	**21.** Answering machine.
_____	**22.** Automatic switch to FAX machine.
_____	**23.** _____
_____	**24.** _____
_____	**25.** _____

Were there one or two features or functions that have you stumped? If your goal is telephone mastery, you know which ones to work on.

4

Contact the office telephone expert. Call the telecommunications department. Find the instruction manual. Make time and take time to master every feature and function of the phone system—even the ones you don't think you'll use. Remember that telephone technology was developed to save time and trouble for the businessperson. The telephone is a business tool. Your job is to know how to use it.

CUSTOMERS, COURTESY, AND YOU

When you answer the telephone in a business, you are interacting with a customer. Every telephone call you make at work gives you an opportunity to strengthen a customer relationship.

You also use the telephone for other reasons too. After all, you may use the telephone to talk to customers at work, but you also talk to colleagues and co-workers on the phone, and they're not customers.

There are really two kinds of customers—external and internal. External ones are the people who call your company to buy products and services. The external customer's call demands your best telephone manners. What about your internal customers?

When you work with other people or you coordinate with other departments or divisions, you are interacting with internal customers. If a colleague calls needing data from you to prepare a report, that person is really your internal customer. Internal telephone calls deserve the same level of courtesy you'd normally use with real customers.

Telephone courtesy should become a habit. Whether you're interacting with external or internal customers, courtesy is always your best telephone strategy.

FOCUS ON TELEPHONE COURTESY

Draw on your own telephone experiences—both as a customer and as a businessperson—to answer the questions below. Then consider each of the related telephone tips.

   1. When you place a call, how many rings do you allow before you assume the party is not going to answer? _____

Tip: To be generous, you'll allow from 4 to 6 rings before you assume the person you are calling is not going to answer.

   2. When the telephone rings, how quickly do you answer? _____

_____

Tip: When you receive a call, answer on the first or second ring. In business the ring of the telephone is not simply an interruption. Answering the telephone is an integral part of your job.

   3. Have you ever been lost when someone tried to transfer your call? _____

Tip: Call transfers are very common. Be sure you know the proper process on your system. Customers who are lost in transfer may become lost business as well. (We will talk more about transferring calls in the next chapter.)

4. When making a business call, do you like being put on hold?

_____

When you're on hold, have you ever felt abandoned or left hanging? _____

Tip: Most people don't like being on hold. Be sure you ask the party if he or she wants to hold. Then check back every 30 seconds to confirm that hold or offer to take a message. Never abandon a caller on hold.

5. Have you ever been on the telephone when the other party dropped the receiver or accidentally banged it on the desktop? __

_____

Tip: It is an unpleasant surprise. Be especially careful in handling the receiver. Your telephone partner will appreciate it.

6. How do you feel when talking on the telephone to someone who is eating or drinking during your conversation? _____

_____

Tip: Don't eat, chew gum, or drink during the conversation. The sounds of consumption are not always pleasant. (Even the sounds associated with cigarette or pipe smoking can be annoying to some people.)

7. What impression do you get when the other person fumbles around looking for a pad or pencil? _____

_____

Tip: You probably imagined the person was not organized or was not very businesslike. Since you always want to make a positive telephone impression, be ready for action. (There's more about handling telephone messages in the next chapter.)

8. When someone says he or she will call back at a specific time—but doesn't—how do you feel? _____

_____

Tip: Telephone tag means two parties try to get in touch by leaving phone messages and attempting callbacks. It's become an irritating fact of business life. If you promise to call back at a certain time, make that call. Likewise, if you've promised to be available at a certain time to receive a call, be there.

9. Suppose you receive a call and are disconnected. Who takes the initiative to resume the call? _____

Tip: The person who made the original call makes the second call to resume an interrupted conversation. The person who received the original call should hang up immediately when the call is disrupted to enable the other party to call back.

4

Chapter Checkpoints

The Importance of Telephone Courtesy

Read the brief telephone call dialogue below. Then answer the questions to describe what's wrong with this example. Check your answers.

Receptionist:

"Young and Miller. [Clank, clatter.] Oops, phone slipped. Sorry about that!"

Caller:

"Oh, hello. I'm Betty Jones with ABC Shoes. I'd like to speak with Mr. Young."

Receptionist:

"Hang on a minute. I'll see if he's in."

Caller:

[Sitting silently on hold for several minutes, tapping her fingers.]

Receptionist:

"Are you still there?" [Sounds of ripping open a bag, followed by crunching.]

Caller:

"Yes. Were you having lunch while I was on hold?"

Receptionist:

[Gulping.] "No, ma'm. Al's not here. You want to call back later?"

Caller:

"I'd like to leave a message . . . On second thought, forget it."

1. What telephone courtesy mistakes were made?

_____

_____

_____

_____

_____

_____

_____

_____

_____

_____

2. What might have happened if the receptionist had been aware of the value of telephone courtesy?

_____

_____

_____

_____

Checkpoint Feedback

Check your responses with those suggested below.

1. Mistakes included the following:

Dropping the phone (line 2).

Not asking the caller if she wanted to be put on hold (line 3).

Using informal language that implied the caller was a bother (line 3).

Leaving the caller on hold too long (line 4).

Annoying sounds (lines 5, 6).

Eating while talking (line 5)

Not offering to take a message (line 7).

2. The caller would not have been annoyed. A customer might have been satisfied instead of disgruntled.

5 | Handling Incoming Calls

This chapter will help you to:

- Handle incoming business telephone calls effectively.
- Place calls on hold and transfer calls courteously.
- Take efficient messages.
- Screen calls tactfully.

ANSWERING THE TELEPHONE

Every time the telephone rings, think of it as an opportunity to do business.

A Prompt Answer

Your first action should be to answer the telephone promptly. If your company does not have a stated policy, assume that the sooner you answer the phone, the better. Answer by the second or third ring, at the latest.

Identify Yourself and Offer Service

Although work situations vary, it's customary to identify your firm, yourself, or your department when you answer an incoming call. It is also an excellent idea to ask how you might help the caller. Consider these examples.

Answering your own telephone:	"Good morning; this is Jerry Jackson. May I help you?"
Answering for the business:	"Good afternoon; USA Bank. Jerry Jackson speaking. How may I assist you?"
Answering for the department:	"Accounting department; Joe Riley speaking. How may I help you?"
Answering for superior or colleague:	"Hello; this is Mr. Long's office; Bob Wilson speaking. May I help you?"

Each situation calls for a slight variation. In each case, the person who answered the call identifies himself or herself, names the business, department, or work group reached, and shows a willingness to assist the caller. Answering calls with this straightforward manner has several benefits. You show your professionalism, present a positive image for your company, and begin to establish rapport.

TAKING ACTION ON INCOMING CALLS

Once you've answered the call, your next steps are to identify the caller and the purpose of the call. Depending on what you find out, typically there are four actions in handling an incoming call.

1. Handle the call yourself (assuming the call is for you).
2. Place the caller on hold.
3. Transfer the call.
4. Take a message.

Some companies have prescribed methods for each of these actions. In others, it's up to the individual to figure out what to do.

Handling the Call

For business telephone calls, the safe route is the conservative one. Use the caller's title and last name (e.g., Mr. Jones, Ms. Reynolds, or Dr. Perkins). Do not operate on a first-name basis unless you are well acquainted with the caller and have established an informal business relationship. Always avoid slang expressions, cliches, or any form of address that might be considered offensive (e.g., honey, dude, dear, guy, man, or kid). You don't want to get the conversation off on the wrong foot.

The same advice applies to closing the call. Use traditional forms of closure such as "good-bye," rather than informal versions like "bye-bye," "so long," or "talk to you later." Typically, you'd expect the caller to make the first signs of closing the call, and you'd stay on the line until the caller has hung up.

Some callers chatter as if you had nothing better to do than visit. This puts the burden of concluding the conversation on you. Here the challenge is to wait for an opening (a breath or other pause), then jump in with a concluding remark, and say good-bye.

Placing a Caller on Hold

Sometimes you need to place the caller on hold. If the requested person is busy on another line or if you need a moment to grab a file, the hold option seems sensible. Be sure to ask if the caller wishes to hold or prefers to leave a message. Here are some examples:

> "Mrs. Browning is talking on another line. Would you care to wait, or may I have her return your call?"

> "Bob Harris is working with another customer at the moment. Would you like to hold, or would you prefer to leave a message? I'm not sure how long he'll be, but it may take some time."

When you put a caller on hold, remember the last time you got stuck. That way, you'll be motivated to check frequently to see if the caller wants to continue to hold or prefers to leave a message or call back. Here are some examples:

> "I'm sorry, but Mr. Jenkins is still on the other line. May I have him return your call later today?"

> "Hello again, Mr. Peele. Ms. Poe expects to be a few minutes longer. Do you want to continue holding, or would you prefer to leave a message?"

Transferring Calls

Often a caller has reached you by mistake and really needs to speak to someone else. That's where call transfer becomes useful. Transfers are routine in business telephone situations, but too many transfers make a negative impression.

When transferring calls, always explain what you are about to do and get the caller's permission. "Mary in the accounts payable department will be able to answer your questions, Mr. Burrows. I'd like to transfer you to her line. Is that all right with you?"

There is always a slight risk that you'll lose the caller when you attempt to transfer. Plan ahead for this possibility. Either get the caller's name and number so you can call back, or be sure the caller has the name and number of the proper contact so he can call back if the transfer is aborted. "Mary in accounts payable is at extension 123. I'll transfer your call now."

Taking Messages

The office seems to be filled with pink slips—those little pink forms designed to make it easy to take telephone messages. The message form is an excellent guide for collecting the right information. A good telephone message enables you to take an appropriate business action in response to the call.

Examine the sample message form below. The form is simple and clear. All you need to do is fill in the blanks, completely and correctly, and then be sure the right person gets the message. The basic questions, who, what, when, why, where, and how, apply to taking messages.

WHILE YOU WERE OUT	
TO _____	
M _____	
OF _____	
PHONE _____	
TELEPHONED	WILL CALL AGAIN
CALLED TO SEE YOU	RETURNED YOUR CALL
WANTS TO SEE YOU	URGENT
PLEASE CALL	VISITED YOUR OFFICE
MESSAGE _____	
DATE _____ TIME _____ AM/PM	
CALL TAKEN BY _____	

Take time to complete the form. Verify the information as you speak with the caller. Check the spelling of names and confirm the phone number and extension.

Detailed Messages.   Suppose you received the following telephone messages. How would you prepare your responses? Which would you handle first?

a. Mr. Jones called. He's in all day today.

b. Ms. Burke returned your call of yesterday.

c. Harry says "go ahead."

d. Betty in marketing wants you to call.

e. Dr. Phillips wants to speak to you about design changes before 5 P.M. today.

Only the last message gives any hint of the caller's real purpose and offers an indicator for prioritizing the responses. You can see what happens when messages are incomplete or lack sufficient information. Always try to determine what issue, request, or need the caller has. Try to estimate the importance or urgency of the call. Your notes in a telephone message will help your co-worker prioritize callbacks and prepare intelligently for them.

Think about It: Handling Incoming Calls

Think about how you currently carry out the four actions for incoming calls. Can you improve in any of those areas? Use the guidelines below to write new action strategies that will work more effectively for your incoming business telephone calls.

1. When I answer my own telephone, I'll say: _____

   _____

2. When I close a telephone conversation, I'll say: _____

   _____

3. When I answer calls for other people (for the department, or for the company), I'll say: _____

   _____

   _____

   _____

   _____

4. When placing a caller on hold, I'll say: _____

_____

_____

_____

5. When I transfer a caller, I'll say: _____

_____

_____

_____

6. When taking messages, I want to make a special effort to: _____

_____

_____

_____

TAKING CALLS FOR SOMEONE ELSE

Many business people prefer handling their own incoming telephone calls, but some situations prevent them from doing so. A writer might be struggling to meet a deadline and want to avoid the interruption of telephone calls. Someone might wish to avoid certain calls and accept others while working on a complex decision. A salesperson may be out making sales calls. A clerk may be in the hospital. For a variety of reasons you may be asked to screen incoming calls for someone else.

These situations always pose a ticklish problem. What do you say to the caller? You don't want to give the impression that the person doesn't want to speak to the caller. You also don't want to give out private information. You need to be tactful and firm.

Screening Calls Tactfully

Here are two sample dialogues. Mr. Pierce is in, but does not want to speak to Mr. Folsom today. Which dialogue makes a more positive impression?

Dialogue Sample A

Bob:

"Good morning. Mr. Pierce's office. Bob speaking."

Caller:

"I want to speak to Mr. Pierce."

Bob:

"Who's calling?"

Caller:

"It's Ray Folsom from the bakery."

Bob:

"Oh, Mr. Folsom, Mr. Pierce is out of the office right now."

Dialogue Sample B

Bob:

"Good morning. Mr. Pierce's office. Bob speaking."

Caller:

"Hello. Is Mr. Pierce there?"

Bob:

"No, he's not available. May I ask who's calling?"

If you chose sample B, you're right. It is both tactful and brief. The first sample seems as though Mr. Pierce might be in—but not for Mr. Folsom.

Protecting Another Person's Privacy

Sally from the shipping department is in the hospital for minor surgery. She has asked Mary to handle her calls. Which is the preferred way to handle this?

Dialogue Sample C

Mary:

"Good afternoon. Finn's Fish Farm."

Caller:

"I'd like to talk to Sally in shipping."

Mary:

"I'm sorry, Sally is not in. May I ask who's calling?"

Caller:

"This is Bill Barton. Where is she, anyway?"

Mary:

"I don't expect her in this week. I'd be pleased to take a message."

Dialogue Sample D

Mary:

"Good afternoon. Finn's Fish Farm."

Caller:

"I'd like to speak to Sally in shipping."

Mary:

"Oh, hadn't you heard? Sally's in the hospital!"

Caller:

"Really? Oh, my . . . . what's the matter?"

Mary:

"I guess Sally had better tell you herself when she gets back."

If you selected sample C, you're right. The challenge here is to protect the other person's privacy in a tactful and businesslike way. It's always a good idea to avoid telephone gossip.

Chapter Checkpoints

Handling Incoming Calls Effectively

For each sample of telephone conversation given below, either write a better one or tell what's wrong with the sample.

1. "Hello. Brady's Hardware."

_____

2. "Sarah's not here. Any message?"

_____

3. "I don't handle inquiries. You'll have to call the warehouse."

_____

4. "How long have you been on hold?"

_____

5. "Good afternoon. This is Mary in accounting."

_____

6. "Good Morning. Ace Investigations; Martha Adams here."

_____

7. "I don't know where Mr. Price is right now."

_____

8. "Ellen's office. Who's calling please?"

_____

9. "Hang on while I try to transfer you."

_____

10. "If I lose you, call the switchboard and we'll try the transfer again."

_____

Checkpoint Feedback

Check your answers with those given below.

1. The person should also give his or her name and state his or her willingness to help the caller.

2. Phrase the information more formally and politely. Courtesy counts.

3. Give the caller the name and extension of the person who can handle inquiries; suggest you transfer the call. Take the initiative for serving the customer.

4. If you have to ask this question, you've made a major error by abandoning the caller. The caller feels unimportant, insulted, and irritated.

5. Mary should also offer to help the caller.

6. Martha might try a more welcoming opening statement. This is grim.

7. If you're answering the phone, you should know where he is. Certainly, you can think of something more professional to say.

8. Identify yourself and wait for the caller to identify himself or herself. Don't rush.

9. This doesn't inspire confidence in the caller. You will transfer—not try.

10. Tell the caller the actual name and number to call, if needed.

6 | Handling Customer Orders

This chapter will help you to:

- Follow a systematic process for handling customer orders.
- Develop an effective strategy for gathering order information.

CUSTOMER ORDERS

Many kinds of business rely on receiving orders over the phone. One example is a company that sells merchandise from a catalog. But there are lots more. What do you order over the telephone? Pizza-to-go, plumbing services, floral arrangements, sports or special events tickets, hotel accommodations, car rentals, groceries, office supplies, and a whole lot more are commonly ordered over the phone.

In each case, someone handles incoming orders. In very large companies, the order-taking process is clearly defined and totally scripted. The order-entry person is trained simply to follow the defined steps. In smaller companies, the process may not be so well structured or training may not be available. The order handler may have to develop an original script.

A General Process for Handling Telephone Orders

The general process for handling telephone orders is simple and straightforward. These three steps are guidelines for call scripting:

First, use a standard opening when you answer the call.

Second, gather and confirm all pertinent order information.

Third, use a reliable method for closing the call.

Let's take a closer look at each step. After you read the tips and suggestions for each step, take time to prepare an appropriate order handling script for your job.

Answering the Call.   When answering the incoming order call, you want to develop and use a standard opening line. This opening should include the following elements: the greeting, the company name, your name, and an offer to help.

> "Good morning. Earthwise Catalog Store. Jean Jones speaking. May I take your order?"

> "Good afternoon. This is Judy at Flowers-by-Wire. How may I help you?"

Your opening:

_____

_____

_____

Gathering and Verifying Order Information.   The second part of the order-handling process is gathering and confirming pertinent order information. In larger firms, the order-handler typically works at a computer terminal that prompts for the information needed in a logical sequence. In other businesses, the order handler uses a form that must be completed. The order form should be used as a guideline for information gathering, but sometimes you need to figure out the most efficient way to complete it.

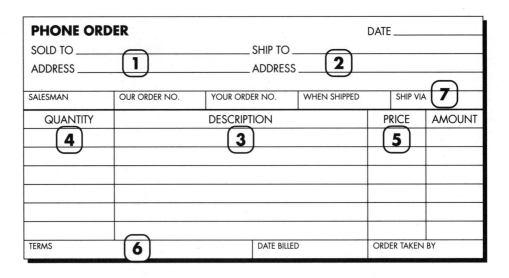

Examine the sample order form shown on the previous page. The numbers on the form indicate the sequence in which the information would be obtained from the customer over the phone. Notice that some areas are not numbered. These items of internal information could be completed before or after the call to save time with the customer.

Now it's your turn to organize order information for efficient capture over the telephone. If you use a standard order form at work, get one now and use it according to the directions given here. (If you don't have an order form, use the sample provided below.) Examine the form carefully and decide which items of information must be captured directly from the customer. Then number those items to establish an appropriate information-gathering sequence. Determine which items, if any, could be filled in before or after the customer call.

6

SERVICE AND REPAIR ORDER   ORDER TAKEN BY _____

DATE RECEIVED _____ TIME _____ AM/PM   NO _____

NAME _____   KIND OF EQUIPMENT _____

ADDRESS _____

DATE PROMISED _____ AM/PM   NAME _____ MODEL _____

TROUBLE OR DEFECT _____	MATERIAL AND PARTS _____		
REMARKS _____			
	LABOR _____		
AUTHORIZED BY	SERVICED BY		
DATE _____	SIGNATURE _____		

Establish a logical sequence for gathering the order information. Ask the ordering questions in the same sequence each time. Stay with your questioning pattern until it becomes an efficient habit. As you gather the order information, take enough time to confirm spelling and verify numerical data. If time permits and the order is short, you may also reconfirm the entire order at the conclusion of the call.

Concluding the Call.   The final step in the order-handling process is concluding the call. As you did with your opening, settle on a standard method of closing the call. Be sure that your closing contains these four elements: a thank-you, a mention of the customer's name, a confirmation of shipping information (if appropriate), and a good-bye.

"Thank you for your order, Mr. Green. You will receive this merchandise in approximately seven working days. Is there anything else I can do for you today? We appreciate your business. Good-bye."

Your closing:

_____

_____

_____

_____

Your Job Is Critical

As the person who handles incoming orders on the telephone, you are your company's first line of customer service. You should exert a positive influence on every customer you handle. If you plan ahead, you know that your opening and closing statements will be appropriate, courteous, and cordial. If you organize your order data for effective information-gathering, you will make your job easier and help the customer place the order correctly. Use *all* your telephone skills.

Hints

Time Out

It used to be that a company used a mail-order catalog to get business. Today, it's not the mail that brings in the orders. It's the telephone.

Chapter Checkpoints

Handling Orders on the Telephone

Check each statement that would make a positive impression on a customer who is placing an order over the telephone.

☐ **1.** "What do you want?"

☐ **2.** "May I confirm the spelling of that street name, please?"

☐ **3.** "What else can I do for you today, Mrs. Wright?"

☐ **4.** "We're delighted to have you as a customer, Mr. Franklin."

☐ **5.** "It's always a pleasure to hear from you, Ms. Hill."

☐ **6.** "Are you ready with the order information yet?"

☐ **7.** "Would you prefer a faster method of shipment?"

☐ **8.** "If you'd talk slower, I could get this stuff right the first time."

☐ **9.** "Thank you for calling Jay's Electric. We appreciate your business."

☐ **10.** "How do you spell that?"

☐ **11.** "Will this be a credit card deal?"

☐ **12.** "Now that we've confirmed the basic order information, Ms. Bryce, tell me the specific items you'd like to order."

☐ **13.** "That item is out of stock. I don't know when it'll be in."

☐ **14.** "We don't have sizes that big."

☐ **15.** "Remember, Mrs. Johnson, we guarantee your satisfaction because we value your business."

Checkpoint Feedback

Check your answers with those given below. Did you mark each of the following as positive statements?

2. "May I confirm the spelling of that street name, please?"

3. "What else can I do for you today, Mrs. Wright?

4. "We're delighted to have you as a customer, Mr. Franklin."

5. "It's always a pleasure to hear from you, Ms. Hill."

7. "Would you prefer a faster method of shipment?"

9. "Thank you for calling Jay's Electric. We appreciate your business."

12. "Now that we've confirmed the basic order information, Ms. Bryce, tell me the specific items you'd like to order."

15. "Remember, Mrs. Johnson, we guarantee your satisfaction because we value your business."

7 | Handling Customer Problems and Complaints

This chapter will help you to:

- Describe the true nature of customer expectations.
- Apply a systematic process for handling customer problems and complaints.
- Create your own standard opening and closing for problem calls.
- Handle a variety of difficult callers.

PROBLEMS AND COMPLAINTS

No matter what your job title or position, you likely handle customer problems or complaints over the telephone. You have internal or external customers. It's not only the telephone salesperson, order-handler, or customer-support representative who faces the challenge of troubleshooting customer problems and complaints on the telephone. It's every person in every job.

When your manager calls to ask you about your budget overruns, or when your co-worker calls to explain a schedule conflict, you are handling a complaint or managing a problem from a customer—an internal customer. As a salesperson, service technician, or support representative, you are the first point of contact between your company and your customers. You handle complaints and manage problems for external customers on a daily basis.

The Challenge of Customer Satisfaction

Handling customer problems and complaints requires a major effort. Sometimes company policy restricts our ability to satisfy legitimate customer concerns. In other cases, the customer's complaint is unwarranted.

Occasionally, customers seem too emotional, almost irrational. Once in a while, the customer is just plain unpleasant. Every incoming telephone call presents a new challenge.

How can you prepare to meet these challenges? Begin by thinking about the customer's expectations.

Customer Expectations

Customers have expectations. Their expectations may involve you, your work, your company, or your company's products and services. On an even broader scale, customers' expectations about how they should be treated are derived from feelings about simple human dignity, social status, and business ethics. Expectations can be quite varied and numerous.

Put yourself into the customer's role. Think about your expectations for a product or service that you purchased recently over the telephone. Suppose you just bought a new television via a telephone call to an electronics warehouse company. Your expectations might have included any of the following:

- A knowledgeable salesperson.
- New (not used or repaired) merchandise.
- Fast, efficient order-taking over the telephone.
- Product warranty.
- Competitive pricing.
- Low-pressure sales tactics.
- Prompt home delivery.
- Being treated cordially and courteously.
- A follow-up call after the sale.

What happens when one or more of these expectations are not met? You'll either call elsewhere to buy, or if you've made the purchase, you'll call to complain.

Although your list of expectations may be completely rational, not every customer's expectations are realistic. Sometimes a customer's expectations are met initially, but later the customer changes expectations. Suppose you bought the TV with a one-year warranty, but two years later you demanded that the company repair the product for free. Some customer expectations can be unreasonable or excessive, but they are still expectations.

Complaints and Problems

When a customer's expectations are not met—for whatever reason—then problems arise. When that happens, the customer may call to voice dissatisfaction or concern. That's where you come in—ready to ensure that the customer's expectations are satisfied.

■ Think about It: How's Your Customer Awareness?

How strong is your customer awareness? Read each statement; then circle Y if you agree or N if you disagree.

Y N   **1.** I believe that the customer is always right.

Y N   **2.** The customer is the most important part of our business.

Y N   **3.** Customers always try to get something for nothing.

Y N   **4.** 100 percent customer satisfaction is my goal.

Y N   **5.** Customers expect me (or my company) to be perfect.

Y N   **6.** Customers typically call with complaints before they have thought through the problem.

Y N   **7.** Customer problems are usually caused by the customer.

Y N   **8.** Most customer expectations are reasonable.

Y N   **9.** I become irritated when a customer is rude.

Y N   **10.** If I can't handle a rude customer, I hang up.

Y N   **11.** In every telephone call, it's me versus them.

Y N   **12.** Customers don't really mind waiting on hold.

Y N   **13.** It doesn't really matter if one or two customers are unhappy.

Y N   **14.** Customers should understand what I am going through at work.

Y N   **15.** Customers tend to blame me for their problems.

7

Are you ready to analyze your results? Check your responses with those given below. Award yourself one point for each response that matches the answer key.

1. Y	6. N	11. N
2. Y	7. N	12. N
3. N	8. Y	13. N
4. Y	9. N	14. N
5. N	10. N	15. N

If you scored from 13 to 15 points: You've got the kind of attitude that will really be an asset in handling customer complaints and problems via the telephone.

If you scored from 11 to 12 points: Remember, every complaint or problem that you handle is an opportunity to make someone happy.

If you scored 10 or less: Develop a positive attitude toward customers. Remember that customers are only people. They're bound to exhibit faults and shortcomings, just like the rest of us.

A LOGICAL APPROACH TO SOLVING PROBLEMS

Handling customer problems and complaints is a difficult job. That's why you need a logical approach, a basic step-by-step process for handling customer complaints and problems.

The Plan

Here is a model for handling customer problems. This model can be used to solve customer problems via the telephone, but the approach itself could be applied to any problem-solving situation.

Look at the process model.

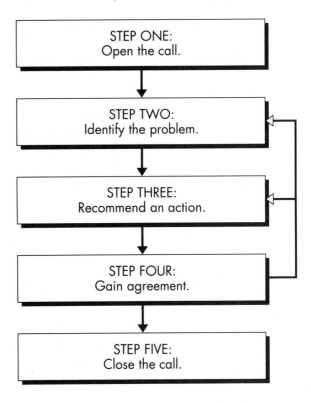

As you read each step, assume that your job requires you to handle incoming telephone calls from customers who have problems, concerns, or complaints.

Step One: Open the Call.   Your objective in opening the conversation is to set a positive tone for the interaction. Use a cheerful expression. Make your voice convey your positive attitude. When answering the telephone, include these items in your opening:

- A greeting.
- Your company name or department name.
- Your name.
- An offer to help the customer.

Note the following example:

"Good Morning. Chandler's Customer Hot Line; Cynthia speaking. How may I help you?"

The proper opening statements and a positive inflection assure the caller of your commitment to service. Your offer to help invites the caller to begin to describe the problem or complaint.

Step Two: Identify the Problem.   At your request, the caller will launch into a description of the problem or complaint. The caller may be calm, rational, and orderly—or just the opposite. The customer may be literate and well-spoken or uneducated and inarticulate. Remember, unhappy customers are dissatisfied. Some may be irritated, angry, and rude. It's your job to sift through all of those complicating emotions to identify the real problem or concern. Here's what you can do to work through this problem-identification step.

- Use your listening skills. Listen carefully for the facts and the underlying attitude. You need to understand the customer's real problem or concern, and you need to recognize the customer's emotional state.
- Apply your questioning skills. Question the customer to uncover details of the problem. Use your skills to confirm your understanding of the problem or complaint.
- Control your own emotions. Always maintain control over your own emotions. Remember that this is a business interaction. If you become personally involved, allow yourself to feel insulted, or lose your temper, you will not last long at the job.
- Keep an open mind. Put yourself in the customer's position. If possible, empathize with the customer's situation.

As you work with the customer to uncover the problem or complaint, let your voice communicate your genuine interest in helping the customer.

Step Three: Recommend an Action.   Suggest a possible solution. The solution should always be in the form of positive action. You might be able to offer the customer a refund, assist the customer in understanding the policy for returned merchandise, or explain how the product works.

When you recommend an action, let your voice show your confidence that this action will resolve the problem. Phrase the recommendation as part of a restatement of the problem as seen in the examples below.

"Mr. Jones, I understand you are unhappy about the delay in receiving your order. If I can guarantee that the order will arrive via air freight no later than Friday, will that meet your needs?"

"Ms. Barker, I'm sorry our service did not meet your standards the first week. I'd like to send the crew out again today, at no charge to you, with more detailed instructions. If the work is satisfactory, would you give us a second chance?"

Step Four: Gain Agreement.   Once you've offered a solution or recommended an action, you need to gain agreement from the customer. As you read the sample action statements, notice that each one ended with a question that asks for the customer's agreement.

If the customer agrees to your solution, you proceed to the last step in this process. If the customer does not agree, then you need to return to a previous step in the process flow. (The white arrows in the flow diagram represent this recycling to an earlier step.) You may have an alternative action to suggest, or you may need to go back to identifying and clarifying the problem or complaint.

What happens when you cannot seem to reach any satisfactory agreement with the customer? In most companies, there will be a trouble-shooting structure that allows you to turn calls over to your supervisor or to specialized customer service representatives who can make additional concessions to the customer.

Step Five: Close the Call.   When the customer agrees to your recommended action, you're ready to close the call. As you close the call, be sure to:

- Confirm the agreed-upon solution or action.
- Thank the customer for calling.
- Indicate willingness to help in the future.

Note the example that follows:

"Your refund check will be processed immediately, Ms. Roberts. You are a valued customer here at House of Hats. If I can be of any assistance with the remainder of your order, please call me."

Let your voice convey your interest in the customer and your belief that you and your company can meet the customer's needs now and in the future.

■ Think about It: Getting Ready for Customer Problems and Complaints

Think about the typical customer complaints or problems that you have to handle on the telephone at work and prepare now.

1. Write your standard opening for incoming customer problem or complaint calls.

_____

_____

_____

2. List the three most common customer complaints or problems that you encounter. For each one, write down the actions that your company permits you to take to resolve the complaint.

Problem: _____

_____

_____

Actions available: _____

_____

_____

Problem: _____

_____

_____

Actions available: _____

_____

_____

Problem: _____

_____

_____

Actions available: _____

_____

_____

3. Write down your standard call closing.

_____

_____

_____

_____

DEALING WITH DIFFICULT CALLERS

The problem-solving process model will give you an excellent foundation for handling customer complaint calls. Unfortunately, there are some callers who are particularly difficult to handle. They require special strategies.

The Angry or Rude Caller

The angry or rude caller can be very intimidating. It is difficult to stand by silently while another person spouts off a tirade or makes unfounded accusations. These callers are on an emotional blitz and can be difficult for anyone to handle.

Your main objective is calming the caller. Until you can get the customer to manage his or her emotions, you won't be able to make any progress. In order to calm the caller, you'll need to work especially hard on:

- Listening patiently.
- Acknowledging the caller's concern.
- Trying to establish a friendly, but businesslike telephone relationship.

Your voice should be calm and comforting. You want to convey your understanding and relate to the customer's concern. The following examples will give you some ideas for defusing the caller's anger.

"I can't blame you for being irritated, Mr. Green. Let me try to solve the problem today—once and for all."

"Mr. Burke, let me apologize on behalf of Bob's Auto Body. I know we agreed to match the paint color on your fender, and we didn't get it right. We'd like to try again, at no cost to you."

"I can certainly understand why you're so upset. There's no excuse for our mistake. Let's work together to remedy the situation."

Depending on how angry the caller is, it may take you more than one try to succeed in calming the caller. Perseverance is part of the job.

Once you've established a more businesslike, less emotional rapport, you can return to a logical point in your standard process model for handling the complaint.

The Talkative Caller

Once in a while, you encounter a customer who simply loves to talk. These customers are wonderfully adept at making small talk. Those customers are using valuable time, and you have calls waiting. What will you do?

First, stifle your normal urge to respond conversationally. Don't chat with the caller just because he or she starts an informal conversation. After the normal opening pleasantries, stick to business matters as much as you can.

A second strategy is to avoid asking any indirect questions. You don't want to encourage the talkative caller to explain, explore, or ramble during the call. Instead, ask specific questions that would minimize the caller's opportunity to stray from the conversational path.

A third strategy might be to quicken your own conversational pace. Limit the breathing room between statements. Move smartly through your line of questioning. Doing so will effectively reduce the caller's ability to interrupt your conversational flow. Beware of overdoing this tactic. If you begin to sound like a fast talker, you've lost your credibility.

When the caller begins to ask you conversational questions, give a very short answer and redirect his or her attention with a service-related question of your own. Here are some examples:

Caller:
"Hello, Bob. Where were you last time I called?

Bob:
"I was on vacation last week. What can I do for you today?"

Caller:

"Hey Buddy! You're probably busy, but I'm going to be out your way soon. Can you recommend a good restaurant in your town?"

Buddy:

"No, I usually eat at home. Is there a technical problem with your system?"

The Hard-to-Understand Caller

Some callers are hard to understand. They may talk too fast or too slowly for you to track their ideas. They may mumble, whisper, mispronounce, or misuse words. Any of these characteristics can make your job more difficult.

Whenever you encounter these situations, you need to address the difficulty immediately and clearly. You need to develop some tactful ways of asking callers to slow down, speed up, talk louder, or speak softer. Here are some examples you might try.

"Mr. Brown, I am having difficulty hearing you. Please speak louder and speak directly into the mouthpiece of your telephone."

"I'm having trouble following your description of events, Mrs. Barrow. Would you start again and speak a little slower?"

"Was it the *collar* you didn't like or the *color*, Mr. Carson?"

The Uncooperative Caller

Sometimes a customer just seems to be uncooperative. Consider these common examples.

Perhaps the caller seems passive, timid, or introverted. In that case, you have to work very hard—probing and nudging to get information from the caller.

Caller:

"I don't really know what happened."

You:

"Why don't you start by explaining what you saw on the screen just before your computer failed."

Perhaps the caller seems assertive because the dialogue is extremely brief and pointed. In that case, be equally assertive and professional to match the caller's tone without being pushy or abrasive.

Caller:

"I wish to speak to someone with the authority to make a decision on this repair issue today."

You:

"I can give you a decision as soon as we confirm your product warranty registration number."

Some callers may seem uncooperative because they are disorganized or disoriented. Draw on your listening and questioning skills to help manage the caller. These calls may require a little more time and effort.

Uncooperative callers can also have a predetermined negative opinion about you or an unrealistic expectation that you cannot accommodate. In this case, make an attempt to resolve the situation yourself, but if the customer persists, call for assistance from your supervisor.

7

Chapter Checkpoints

Key Ideas

In your own words, describe each of the steps in the process model for handling customer problems or complaints. When you've finished your descriptions, review the plan on the previous pages to check your answers.

Step One: Open the call.

_____

_____

_____

Step Two: Identify the problem.

_____

_____

_____

_____

_____

_____

_____

Step Three: Recommend an action.

_____

_____

_____

_____

Step Four: Gain agreement.

_____

_____

_____

_____

Step Five: Close the call.

_____

_____

_____

Mark each statement T or F.

T F   **1.** A customer's expectations are always reasonable.

T F   **2.** Complaints and problems may arise from either internal or external customers, or both.

T F   **3.** Customer expectations may involve the company, the product, general business ethics, human relations—almost anything.

T F   **4.** Having a positive attitude is an essential part of handling customer problems and complaints effectively.

T F   **5.** In step one of the problem-solving process, your goal is to set a positive tone for the call.

T F   **6.** In step two of the problem-solving process, your goal is to identify and confirm the customer's concern, problem, or complaint.

T F   **7.** In step three of the problem-solving process, your goal is to suggest or recommend an action that will resolve the problem.

T F   **8.** In step four of the problem-solving process, your goal is to gain agreement from the customer that the suggested action will satisfy the customer's needs.

T F   **9.** In step five of the problem-solving process, your goal is to confirm your agreement and close the call.

T F   **10.** Listening and questioning skills are particularly important in steps one and five of the problem-solving process.

T F   **11.** To calm an irate caller, you can acknowledge the concern and apologize in a general way, if needed.

T F   **12.** To manage the talkative caller, you should try to ask only indirect questions.

T F   **13.** Handle a hard-to-understand caller by pretending everything is OK.

Checkpoint Feedback

Check your answers.

1. F
2. T
3. T
4. T
5. T
6. T
7. T
8. T
9. T
10. F
11. T
12. F
13. F

8 | Handling Outbound Calls

This chapter will help you to:

- Describe the main types of outbound business calls.
- Develop a customized script for your own outbound calls.
- Interact efficiently with voice-mail and messaging systems.

OUTBOUND CALLS

It's time to turn things around. So far, you've been working on handling incoming calls. Now, the topic is making outbound calls. Most outbound calls fall into one of two categories: initiating or following up on a business action.

Hello, Would You? . . .

Outbound calls frequently initiate a business action. For example, you might make a business telephone call to:

- Sell something.
- Gather information.
- Set up appointments.
- Make travel arrangements.
- Plan meetings and schedule events.
- Provide information.

Hello, May I? . . .

Outbound calls are also used to follow up business actions. For example, you've probably made outbound calls to:

- Assure customer satisfaction.
- Provide customer service after a sale.
- Explain and resolve mistakes.
- Respond to requests.
- Confirm information or make changes.

HOW TO SUCCEED WITH OUTBOUND CALLS

What's the secret of success for outbound calls? If you've been working steadily through this book, then the secret may be no surprise. It's planning—plain and simple.

You used a clear, practical planning process when you prepared for handling customer problems and complaints. You did the same kind of systematic planning for handling orders. Outbound calling is no exception. Outbound calls become more manageable if you plan them.

No matter what kind of outbound call you're making, here is an outline to use as a planning guide.

1. Greet the customer and identify yourself.
2. State the reason for your call.
3. Present your message or ask your questions.
4. Confirm understanding or gain agreement.
5. Closing for the call.

The outline should seem familiar. It's similar to some of the process models and flows you covered earlier. Here's a sample dialogue that follows the outline. Can you locate each of the five items in the sample? Write the number of the item in the margin next to the appropriate bit of conversation.

Mary:
"Hello, Ms. Grant. This is Mary Allen from the Western Regional Office."

Ms. Grant:

"Hi, Mary. What's up?"

Mary:

"I'm calling to ask you to attend a training seminar here next week. All of the branch managers are invited. It's next Friday, 8 AM to 5 PM. Will you be able to attend?"

Ms. Grant:

"Let me check my calendar . . . yes, I could attend."

Mary:

"Excellent. I'll send you a meeting agenda and travel plan immediately via fax."

Ms. Grant:

"OK, Mary. Count me in."

Mary:

"Thank you, Ms. Grant. I look forward to seeing you next week. If you have any questions, just give me a call. Good-bye."

■ Think about It: Planning Your Outbound Calls

8

All you have to do to make successful outbound calls is plan them.

1. What kinds of outbound business calls do you typically make?

   _____
   _____
   _____
   _____
   _____
   _____

2. Choose one outbound business call and prepare for it.
   Opening:_____

   _____

   Reason for call:_____

   _____

   _____

   Message and questions:_____

   _____

_____
_____
_____
_____
_____
_____
_____

Confirm understanding and gain agreement:_____

_____
_____

Close:_____

_____

■ **H i n t s** ─────────────────────────

Time Out

Time out . . . for some career advice. There is one kind of outbound call that you don't want to make at work. Do you know what it is? It's the *personal* call.

If you must make a personal call during the business day, make it at a telephone away from your desk (preferably a pay phone away from the office) and during your break or lunch hour.

ANSWERING MACHINES AND VOICE-MAIL SYSTEMS

We've all had a variety of experiences with answering machines and voice-mail systems. For some, they are terrific time-savers; for others, they are a bother. When these hi-tech systems work, they are applauded. When they don't, they can do more harm than good. Telephone answering systems are here to stay, and you need to learn how to interact with them.

Sometimes the machine doesn't work quite right or doesn't allow enough time to leave a coherent message. Sometimes we're caught by surprise and forced to stumble and stammer our way through an ineffective message. The telephone-answering system is a good reason to plan your outbound calls.

"Please Leave a Message . . . ."

Here are some helpful hints:

- Plan the call. Be ready with two alternatives: a detailed message for systems that permit you to talk longer, and a brief message for those that don't.
- When the system answers, listen carefully for directions. Some systems are user-friendly, but others are not.
- Always identify yourself immediately.
- Tell the day or date and time you are leaving the message.
- Give some indication of the urgency of your message.
- Speak clearly and concisely.
- If you want a callback (or you will call again), say so and give the day and time when you'd like that to occur.
- State your telephone number.

8

"When You Hear the Tone . . . ."

If you have an answering machine or voice-messaging system at work, prepare a welcome, offer directions, and manage your incoming voice-mail. Here are some tips:

- Learn to use your system.
- Keep your answering statement brief.
- As a rule, answer your phone when you are at your desk. Most callers hate to feel they're being screened.
- When away from your desk, update your answering statement frequently, if possible.
- If you are going to be away for a day or more, leave a message that refers callers to someone else who may be able to help them.
- Check your messages frequently.
- Respond to messages promptly.

8

Think about It: Mind over Machine

Telephone-answering technology requires a sense of humor. Which of these answering-system nightmares has happened to you?

- ☐ Got cut off in mid-sentence trying to leave a message.
- ☐ Made a mistake in the message, called back, and left another.
- ☐ Waited for the beep that never came.
- ☐ Couldn't understand the name of the person who left you the message and didn't recognize the voice.
- ☐ Forgot to review messages and missed an important one.
- ☐ A power or equipment failure garbled all your messages.
- ☐ Didn't realize your answering statement had been obliterated.
- ☐ Forgot to erase messages and had no idea which were current.
- ☐ Erased messages you wish you'd saved.
- ☐ Offended a good customer by screening calls.
- ☐ Left a detailed message for someone, then accidentally canceled or erased it by pushing the wrong button.

These situations are laughable, until they happen to you. You have no control over people who leave you messages, but with planning you can avoid most of these problems. For each item you checked above, form a plan that will prevent it from happening again.

8

Chapter Checkpoints

Scripting an Outbound Call

Script an outbound call right now. Call Mr. Brown to tell him that you underestimated the cost of remodeling his kitchen. Instead of costing $4,800 as you originally said, it will be $5,100. (You verified materials costs and were shocked to discover recent price increases in cabinetry.)

Write a script for the call. Refer to the outline and sample on pages 72–73.

Checkpoint Feedback

There is no single correct script for this scenario. If your script includes the five outline items and is courteous and clear, it will probably work fine. Here is one possible script.

You:

"Good Morning, Mr. Brown. This is Rudy with R&R Construction."

Mr. B:

"Oh, hi, Rudy."

You:

"Mr. Brown, I'm calling to explain an embarrassing mistake."

Mr. B:

"Oh, really? What's wrong?"

You:

"After I quoted you a price of $4,800 for your kitchen remodeling job, my supplier told me there has been a recent price hike on the cabinets you selected. That adds another $300 to your costs. Your job will now be $5,100, instead of $4,800."

Mr. B:

"Gosh—that's more than I had budgeted."

You:

"I apologize for the error in my bid, Mr. Brown. However, if you want those cabinets, we've got to cover the extra cost. On the other hand, you may wish to consider another type of cabinet."

Mr. B:

"Let me think about this today. I'll call you back tomorrow with my decision."

You:

"That'll be fine, Mr. Brown. And thank you for being so understanding. Good-bye."

Telephone Skills Inventory

Mark each item T or F.

T F   **1.** The telephone is the most popular means of communication in business.

T F   **2.** Human communication is a process whereby information is transferred from one person to another.

T F   **3.** Telephone skills are totally different from traditional communication skills.

T F   **4.** A communication model usually includes a sender, a message, a channel, and a receiver.

T F   **5.** If the communication model is applied to the telephone, the sender is the speaker and the receiver is the telephone itself.

T F   **6.** The three key skills of listening, questioning, and speaking are involved in every telephone call you make.

T F   **7.** A conversation implies a two-way exchange of information.

T F   **8.** In an average telephone conversation, you should spend about 50 percent of your time listening.

T F   **9.** Listening is the same as hearing.

T F   **10.** There are serious risks associated with a failure to listen during a business telephone call.

T F   **11.** Listening should be an active skill, not a passive one.

T F   **12.** Direct questions are designed to obtain specific pieces of information.

T F   **13.** Indirect questions are used to uncover opinions, ideas, or general information.

T F   **14.** Direct questions are only used during telephone sales calls.

T F   **15.** During telephone conversations, it's best to avoid asking indirect questions.

T   F   16. Your questioning skills will be needed to confirm or verify information over the telephone.

T   F   17. Pitch, speed, and volume are factors that influence the speaking voice.

T   F   18. Inflection is the modulation or change in a speaker's pitch or tone.

T   F   19. A voice without inflection is called a monotone.

T   F   20. Your general goal is to develop a speaking voice that is professional and businesslike on the telephone.

T   F   21. Every business telephone call you make is an opportunity to strengthen or weaken a customer relationship.

T   F   22. Internal customers are those that actually come to your store or business to make their purchases.

T   F   23. Telephone courtesy suggests that you answer on the first or second ring, but you let the phone ring four to six times when you are calling someone.

T   F   24. It's acceptable business procedure to place and leave a caller on hold for up to 15 minutes.

T   F   25. When taking messages for someone else, always try to determine what issue, request, or need the caller has.

T   F   26. All customer expectations are reasonable.

T   F   27. A customer whose expectations are not met will not be a satisfied customer.

T   F   28. As a telephone order-taker, you are your company's first-line interface with its customers.

T   F   29. In handling customer complaints or problems, identify the problem, recommend an action, and then get the customer's agreement.

T   F   30. If a customer is rude during a telephone call, you can be too.

T   F   31. If a customer wants to chat—no matter how long— you should continue the conversation pleasantly.

T   F   32. If a customer is hard to understand over the telephone, address the difficulty immediately and clearly.

T   F   33. If you are not able to handle a customer complaint effectively, or if the caller is not responding to your efforts, you should refer the caller to your supervisor.

T F   34. To calm an irate caller, acknowledge the concern and apologize in a general way.

T F   35. Having a positive attitude is an essential part of handling customer problems and complaints over the telephone.

If you scored 30 or less: Consider reviewing key content.

If you scored 31 to 35: You've mastered the key ideas.

If you scored 36 to 39: You've done a terrific job.

							35. T
	33. T	**34. T**					
32. T	**31. F**	**30. F**	**29. T**	**28. T**	**27. T**	**26. F**	**25. T**
24. F	**23. T**	**22. F**	**21. T**	**20. T**	**19. T**	**18. T**	**17. T**
16. T	**15. F**	**14. F**	**13. T**	**12. T**	**11. T**	**10. T**	**9. F**
8. T	**7. T**	**6. T**	**5. F**	**4. T**	**3. F**	**2. T**	**1. T**

Check your answers, and total the correct answers.

ANSWER KEY

Post-Test

Find out how good you are! First, analyze your business telephone skills with this personal inventory. If you find that you can't score a 4 or 5 on each item, take time to review these skills. Then, develop a personalized improvement plan using the Skill Maintenance checklist at the end of this book.

For each skill listed, circle a number to estimate your own skill level.

5 = Excellent, 4 = Very good, 3 = Good, 2 = Fair, 1 = Poor

Listening

1 2 3 4 5   1. Listening for understanding.
1 2 3 4 5   2. Verifying what you think you heard.
1 2 3 4 5   3. Listening for expression.
1 2 3 4 5   4. Listening for what is not being said.
1 2 3 4 5   5. Listening objectively.

Questioning

1 2 3 4 5   6. Staying involved in the telephone conversation.
1 2 3 4 5   7 Formulating appropriate questions.
1 2 3 4 5   8. Using direct questions effectively.
1 2 3 4 5   9. Using indirect questions effectively.
1 2 3 4 5   10. Listening to answers given.

Speaking

1 2 3 4 5   11. Keeping voice pitch at low-to-middle range.
1 2 3 4 5   12. Speaking at a medium speed.
1 2 3 4 5   13. Speaking at a medium volume.
1 2 3 4 5   14. Using inflection to give your voice personality.
1 2 3 4 5   15. Speaking clearly.

Telephone Tips, Courtesy, and Incoming Calls

1 2 3 4 5   16. Using all telephone features properly.
1 2 3 4 5   17. Responding courteously to customers on the telephone.
1 2 3 4 5   18. Answering promptly.
1 2 3 4 5   19. Using hold appropriately.
1 2 3 4 5   20. Transferring calls efficiently.

1 2 3 4 5   21. Taking effective messages.
1 2 3 4 5   22. Identifying yourself immediately.
1 2 3 4 5   23. Screening calls tactfully.
1 2 3 4 5   24. Protecting another person's privacy.
1 2 3 4 5   25. Offering to help.

Handling Customer Orders on the Phone

1 2 3 4 5   26. Using a standard opening.
1 2 3 4 5   27. Gathering order information.
1 2 3 4 5   28. Verifying order information.
1 2 3 4 5   29. Using a standard closing.
1 2 3 4 5   30. Keeping a friendly, businesslike telephone manner.

Handling Customer Problems and Complaints

1 2 3 4 5   31. Setting a positive tone for the conversation.
1 2 3 4 5   32. Identifying the customer's problem, concern, or issue.
1 2 3 4 5   33. Remaining cool and collected.
1 2 3 4 5   34. Recommending an action to solve the problem.
1 2 3 4 5   35. Gaining customer agreement.
1 2 3 4 5   36. Handling irate or angry callers.
1 2 3 4 5   37. Handling talkative callers.
1 2 3 4 5   38. Handling hard-to-understand callers.
1 2 3 4 5   39. Handling uncooperative callers.
1 2 3 4 5   40. Achieving customer satisfaction.

Making Outbound Calls

1 2 3 4 5   41. Greeting the customer and stating reason for call.
1 2 3 4 5   42. Presenting message/asking questions.
1 2 3 4 5   43. Confirming understanding.
1 2 3 4 5   44. Using your voice-mail system effectively.
1 2 3 4 5   45. Leaving voice-mail messages for others.

THE BUSINESS SKILLS EXPRESS SERIES

This growing series of books addresses a broad range of key business skills and topics to meet the needs of employees, human resource departments, and training consultants.

To obtain information about these and other Business Skills Express books, please call Business One IRWIN toll free at: 1-800-634-3966.